Minimalist Money Management

Contents:

Conclusion

Introduction:

Are you in debt right now? Are you perhaps living over and beyond your means? Are you constantly worried about money? Are you completely stressed out? Unfortunately we live in a world where most people would answer yes to all four of those questions. We've been lead to believe that the more you have the more that you are as a person, and the more you will be loved by those around you. We want things even when we have so much and we are constantly unhappy with our lives. We sometimes subconsciously believe that our possessions will make us happy and so we buy even when we don't need to or when we cannot afford it. We accumulate credit card after credit card. We use one credit card to pay off the other and so the cycle continues.

We're here to tell you that you can make an awesome but simple change and finally get yourself out of that debt. Taking control over your finance doesn't have to be as hard as you think and with a few small changes done consistently and good habits you'll find yourself finally in a place of financial freedom. By the time you finish this book you will feel so much more at ease knowing that you are making incredible progress toward a simpler financial life every single day. This book may even spark some creativity, leading you to come up with even more ways to cut spending and maximize the value of your money. We seek not just to change your spending habits, but rather to inspire a new shift in mind-set– a mind-set that leads to a sense of empowerment and confidence when it comes to money matters.

We live in a society today where money tends to control people. There are even car bumper stickers that say "I owe, I owe, so off to work I go." Whether or not they will admit it, most people have trouble with money and they feel out of control of their finances; enslaved by the credit card companies and by the debts they have accrued over time. There's got to be a reason they call it 'financial freedom' after all. It's time to take that control back. Using the simple tips and tricks in this book, we will set you on a path of achieving financial peace of mind, if not complete freedom. By using these tactics, your mind will shift in turn, and minimalist money management will become a habit. Over time you will be one of the incredibly few people in control of their finances and not the other way around. And that is so powerful!

Thank you for reading, and I hope by the end you feel excited about starting a new stress-free, financially-free life.

Chapter 1: Benefits

Before we take you through HOW you can live a debt free and minimalistic life, we are going to give you a better understanding of WHY you should do it.

Benefit #1: You'll have less and yet have more.

By streamlining your life you'll have less material things, and yet you'll feel like you have gained so much more. You'll have more space, more time and more money to do the things you really want to do. You'll finally understand the sentiment of 'less is more' and you'll stop looking for happiness in all the wrong places. You'll finally be at peace with who you are. You'll feel a bigger sense of freedom wash over you. It may seem strange to you now, because there are probably so many things that you want and that you wish you had, and that you feel deep down would make you truly happy. Getting out of this mind set and head space is certainly not easy, but once you finally get out of that way of thinking you'll find you open your mind up to so many more amazing things. You'll see truth in what is important and what is not. When you're older and you're looking back on your life, you won't remember what model of phone you had or how big your house or television set was. Instead you'll remember your family, the friends you had and the experiences that you shared together. Sometimes it's important to just take a step back and see life for what it truly is.

Benefit #2: You'll have money for when it counts.

You'll save money. By having less and minimalizing your life, you'll finally be able to save money because you won't be wasting it on unnecessary things. Because of this you'll actually have extra money for when you need it. When you learn to spend money in the right way you'll find that you end up saving so much more than you used to. You'll be surprised at just how much more you are able to save each month, and you'll finally be able to go on the holidays you want or have money for your health and other important issues. Most people live from pay check to pay check and never have enough money to save. By going debt free you'll finally be able to save money and create an important emergency fund to spend when you most need it. You'll feel proud about the money you have saved and enjoy it so much more when you do get to spend it. Yearly holidays finally can become something of a reality instead of a pipe dream. You'll also have the feeling of security knowing that if anything goes wrong, if you lose your job or if you suddenly and urgently need money, that you'll actually have something to fall back on. That feeling of security is a welcome relief to be able to fall back on when you need it.

Benefit #3: You'll find more gratitude in the small things.

When you have too much, or when you constantly want more, you end up becoming desensitized to the things that you already have. You stop seeing what is already around you and you become ungrateful. You believe that you'll only be happy when you have certain things but when you get them then you just look towards the next best thing. By taking a more minimalistic approach to your life and by taking control over your money and your savings, you'll finally see your life for what it is. You'll find gratitude in everything you already have and appreciate the things in your life. You'll finally find joy in your life that was actually always there to begin with and you'll wonder why you never saw it before. You will become more open and more susceptible to the positive things in life.

Benefit #4: You'll be less stressed and more focused.

One of the biggest causes of stress is money issues. Being in debt causes stress, and stress leads to many emotional and physical problems. It becomes a bit of a catch 22 situation because the stress causes health issues, and the health issues need money to solve them, and so the circle continues. By taking control over your money situation and finally finding ways to save and improve your life, you'll find yourself become less and less stressed. You'll be more focused and you'll finally feel as if you are the master of your own fate. You'll get sick less, and therefore have less to spend on your health. You'll be happier and freer than you've ever felt before. Stress effects many parts in your life, and you'll find that by being stressed you actually effect the way you eat, sleep and think. You'll eat incorrectly, you'll sleep poorly and you'll have a very negative outlook on life. Sorting out your stress related issues, such as your money problems, will benefit the entire way you live your life.

Benefit #5: Your relationships will grow.

It is a well-known fact that one of the biggest concerns in a relationship is money. Money can literally break down a once solid relationship and cause it to fail. When you stop seeing money as your only way of finding happiness you'll finally realize that it actually has no control over you at all. It's a man-made object that can be accumulated and grown just as much as it can be used and spent. You'll find ways to take control over your own money and become smart in your buying purchases. You'll be able to save and you'll find that money stops getting in the way of every argument that you have with your partner. You'll finally have the time and the resources to concentrate wholly on your own relationship rather than let money get in the way of what's really important. You relationships will flourish.

Benefit #6: You'll have more freedom.

You're in debt and you somehow come across some money, perhaps through a job or through winnings. Well the first thing you do is you put it towards paying up your debt, and suddenly the money has vanished. Without debt you have the freedom to do whatever you want with that money, whether that means saving it or buying something for yourself or even going on holiday. The freedom to do what you want when you are debt free is one of the greatest benefits of all. When you are in debt you feel constantly confined.

Benefit #7: You'll feel better about yourself.

Being in debt can be quite soul destroying. You feel guilty about how far you let things get and you become completely overwhelmed at where you went wrong. Most people in debt think very poorly of themselves. Becoming debt free means you can finally take control over your own life again. It means you'll be proud of yourself and happy about where you are in your life. It's a great feeling of self-accomplishment.

Benefit #8: You'll pass on good habits to others.

People learn by what you do and not by what you say, especially children. Being debt free and being in control of your financial life is a great thing to pass on to your children, and a great thing to show to those around you. By showing them how you can live a good life without being in debt will help them to cultivate the same good habits.

Chapter 2: 31 Tips and Tricks

So now that we've shown you WHY you should live a debt free and self-sufficient life, we're going to show you HOW to do it, through 30 tips and tricks. While not all of these may apply to you, most of these should be able to help you through your journey of becoming debt-free. Remember that it's all about the small changes that you do that will help to create a more mindful way of living. These small changes will eventually lead to you getting to a place in your life where you need to be. Debt-free and doing the things you have always wanted to do. It IS possible and we're here to show you how.

Tip #1: Credit Card – You only need the one

Do you remember how exciting it was to get your first credit card? That moment that it became approved and you had the shiny new card in your hand, ready and waiting to spend on whatever you wanted? You suddenly felt that buying things was finally in your reach rather than a distant dream. You promised yourself that you would never max it out and that you would only use it when you absolutely had to. You made your first purchase, and then a second, and then suddenly your credit card was maxed out. It happened way faster than you ever thought possible and you felt ashamed for every having laughed at other people for doing the same. But now that your credit card is maxed out you have a problem because you have no money and no fall backs. So you get another credit card to help with the last one. Soon your debts have grown and you find yourself unable to survive with a good few credit cards constantly at hand. While credit cards are handy to have, and certainly good for credit records, you do NOT need more than one, and you need to start working your way towards paying them off. This is possible, however you have to realize that it won't just happen overnight.

Let's look at a few steps that you can take towards making yourself credit card free:

- Increase your monthly payment so that you are paying more than you have been. This will speed up the rate in which your payments are paid off. Remember that the lower your debt on your card is, the less your monthly repayments will be, so this is an important step to take. This is when most of you will say that you do not have the money to pay back more than you have to, however this is not the case. For now, find one thing you can give up in order for you to have extra money to pay back your credit card. This might simply be that you don't go out for dinner for a while. Whatever it is that you can sacrifice, remember that you are doing it all towards the greater good on becoming debt free.
- Don't keep all your cards in your wallet. If you have your cards readily available at all time then you'll more than likely use them. Then when you have cleared your debt, cancel the credit cards that you don't need.

- Once you have your credit card debt in check, from now on make sure you pay off your credit card balance in full every month. This will improve your credit score a lot if you do this consistently.
- For each credit card you pay off, cut it up and close the account! You now have fewer bills to pay every month, and more money in your pocket! Paying off credit cards has an incredible compounding effect. It becomes easier to pay off other debts with each debt you pay off completely. You will feel so much more at ease after you pay off your first card and want to continue making progress! The best place to start is with your lowest balance. Pay that off to build momentum!

Tip #2: Be shop smart

Do you know how much money you spend when you go shopping or do you simply go to the store whenever you feel like it and grab whatever takes your fancy at the time? Most people will not be able to tell you exactly what they bought because they haven't really given the process much thought. They have no idea what they are eating throughout the week so they just take whatever looks good to them at the shop, and then when they realize they don't have enough ingredients on the day they are cooking they go back to buy more. They forget to check what they already have in the cupboards and end up buying far more than they need, including many items that simply go to waste. I know far too many people that end up throwing away food at the end of each week simply because they failed to plan. If you want to be shop smart then you have to think carefully about the shopping process and make sure that you are buying what you need, and ONLY what you need. To do this you need to know exactly what you have at home and what needs topping up. You need to decide (even if it's only roughly) what you'll be eating throughout the week so that you can buy the ingredients for those meals. Then lastly you need to visit the shop with a list of exactly what you need and then buy only from that list without deviating at all. This will stop you from coming home with things that you already have at home, things that you don't need, or things that you bought simply because you shopped on a whim. And if you want to make sure you don't buy all the chocolates or sweets in sight, then make sure you don't go shopping when you are hungry. Shopping when hungry is the surest way to come home with a basket filled with things you really should not have purchased. Be smart when you shop and you won't waste your money each week!

Tip #3: Know the sales

Sales are a great way of saving money on items that you were going to buy anyway from the shops. Sales are bad if you are simply buy items that are cheap and then end up coming home with bags filled with things you didn't really want. It's all about looking to see if any of the items that you need on your list are actually on sale, even if that means buying a different brand to what you normally buy. It's about keeping in touch with shops through social media or newsletters and knowing exactly when and what the sales are each week. If you go to the shops frequently enough, you may notice patterns in when items you particularly buy go on sale. It might happen on a specific day of the week every week (because they have to move in new inventory). You'll be surprised at how much you can save if you simply know which sales the shops are having. If a sale item is not on your list but it's something you buy very often and can easily be stored in a cupboard for months to come, then this would be a good purchase to get and not to ignore. This is one time you can deviate off from your list because it will save you money in the long run. Know your sales, use your coupons and use your discount cards. It may not seem a lot at the time but remember that every single bit of saving adds up to a greater sum at the end.

Tip #4: Don't shop on an empty stomach

You may have noticed that when you go to the shops for groceries when you are hungry that everything in the store looks far more tasty. The hungrier you are the worse this effect can be. As you may be able to imagine, because everything looks so darn good, you will be much more likely to buy things that aren't on your grocery list or perhaps more than what's on your grocery list. So before you go shopping, make sure you have had plenty to eat. I have a theory that the more full you are when you go shopping, the less you spend. I don't recommend eating until you burst of course, but if you are slightly more than satisfied, odds are you will be less inclined to buy more food while at the shops.

Tip #5: Your home doesn't have to be big

Most people dream of living in a huge house, with plenty rooms and tons of storage space. They want a lounge, an office, rooms for all the children, rooms for themselves, rooms for guests, rooms for crafts, a big kitchen, a dining room, a study, an outside area, etc. However all of this is not necessary at all, and while you don't all have to cram in one small room, you certainly don't need as much space as you think you do. I've been living in a small space for quite some time now and I've realized that it's the perfect way to stop spending money on unnecessary things. We have the right amount of bedrooms for the amount of people that live here; we have a kitchen, a lounge and a bathroom. We don't have any 'extras' and nothing is too big. The good thing about this is that we don't buy things that we don't need simply because we do not have the space to keep them. So instead, we use our money on the things that matter. We use some on experiences, and some we put towards our emergency fund. We actually have the money to do the things we want to do and we have learnt to find value in the things that truly matter in life. We feel good in the home that we live in because it's homely and completely uncluttered, giving us the perfect amount of space to feel good in. Most people choose to live beyond their means simply because this is what they have been lead to believe is what society thinks is good.

Tip #6: Before buying, ask yourself 'do I really need this?'

One of the best tips someone gave me was to pick up every item whenever I went shopping for anything and ask myself honestly if it's something I really need. A lot of the time it's something you simply want, but that you don't necessarily need. Of course, this is not always a bad thing. Buying something because you want it will happen and you certainly shouldn't have to deny yourself of everything that comes your way. But be honest with yourself and don't succumb to simply buying too often "just because". You'll just end up with a lot of things that you didn't really need in the first place. If I want something but don't need it then I walk away and think about it before buying it. If, after I've given it some good amount of time and thought, I still want to get it and if it's within my means to do so, then I will. Otherwise I'll walk away. Your needs come first. Remember also that especially when you are trying to rid yourself of debt, to be as ruthless as possible when it comes to your buying choices. You'll start to buy with a lot more thought than before, and you'll start to see which items hold true value and which are there to just reel you in for a short while.

Tip #7: Name brands are NOT important

I like people for who they are and not for what they are wearing, and you should feel the same about what people think of you. If someone dislikes you simply because you are not wearing a certain name brand then they don't really seem like someone you should be making too much time for anyway. We spend far too much time worrying about things like this that make absolutely no difference in our lives anyway. You can look good without a name brand, and you can save money in the process. The same goes for many non-clothes related items. Some people buy things for themselves or for their home because of the brand and because of the stigma that is attached to that brand. They will do this even though they can find the same item, without a brand name, at a cheaper cost. They are only doing this because they want to portray themselves in an opulent way. The truth is that nobody really cares about what you have. They (should) only care about who you are.

Additionally, avoid name brands on things other than clothing. Whether it is in the food shops or at the pharmacy, you can save yourself a lot of money simply by purchasing the non-name brand item. Nearly every supermarket has a brand of its own and its almost always less expensive than name brand and odds are it is as good as the name brand product. For the most part, when you are buying name brand of anything you are paying for the fancy label more so than the product itself.

Tip #8: Drink coffee at home

This was one of the hardest things for me to do because going out for my morning cup of coffee was one of my favourite things to do. Especially when an amazing café was simply down the road from me. I went so often that they knew me by name and had my coffee ready for me as soon as I walked in. This was great. The problem was that I was spending far too much money on something that I could easily make myself at home, and I'd often end up buying a bite to eat at the same time simply because I was right there and it was in front of me. I made the decision to stop going and to instead learn how to make good coffee for myself at home. The amount of money I saved on something so simple was incredible, and the reason that I knew how much I saved was because each day I'd put that money aside into a jar. Three months later and I had saved quite a decent amount of cash, which I put to a far better use. Think of it this way: if you spend $3 for a latte every day for a whole year, you will have spent $1,095, so this is a fantastic way to cut costs. Don't get me wrong, I still treat myself every now again because cafes are still one of my favourite places to go to, but I now enjoy it so much more because I'm not doing it every day. This made me realize how just small decisions and habits can completely change the amount of money you spend and the amount that you save.

Tip #9: Cash is king

Most people walk around with no cash on them, because using a card has simply become easier and more convenient. The problem with cards is that even though you are paying and money is coming off them, you don't physically see it happen. Because of this the brain doesn't register as well as if you had paid in cash, and you're almost fooled to believe that you didn't spend anything. It's also far easier to lose track of what money you have spent on your card then if you were to use actual cash. Research has shown that when a person spends cash versus credit, the pain centers in the brain activate to a higher degree. It is physically more painful to spend with cash! Therefore, you'll be less inclined to hand over a wad of money than you would be should you use a card, because actually seeing the money leaving your hand might make you think twice about a purchase. This is not to say you have to carry around all your money on your, but rather to try to use cash as often as you can. If you are buying something and you don't have the money on you then look for an ATM and draw the money yourself. The more you can pay in cash, the better. You'll be surprised at what a simple change such as this can do for you. Cash is king.

Tip #10: Have a monthly budget

Having a monthly budget is by far one of the greatest money saving tips you will ever get. Knowing exactly what your budget is each month will ensure that you do not by anything that is unnecessary. Of course, emergencies happen and for that there should always be an emergency fund that you can turn to. If you do not have a budget than you do not have a limit as to how much you can spend and it's then very easy to go far beyond what you should be spending. The best way to draw up a budget is to first keep a list of everything you have spent for a few months and to look at what cut backs you could've made throughout those weeks. Also make a list of what you have to spend money on, whether that be rent or food, so that you know exactly what needs to go into your budget each month. Once you know exactly what you need each month you can draw up a monthly budget to help you each month in each of these areas of spending. Anything beyond that is a luxury that is not needed. Remember to include a savings section in your budget so that you can start to build up your savings plan each month. Ask yourself 'what can I cut back on so that I can have more money to put towards my savings?'.

Tip #11: Know where your money is going

It's important to be mindful about where your money is going each month. The best way to do this is to keep a spread sheet and to write down every time you buy something. While this is easy for the bigger purchases, it can be quite daunting for the small purchases. So what you can do is keep a box on your desk and throw in your slips at the end of each day. Then at the end of each week you can add that to your spread sheet. You'll be amazed at how many small and unnecessary things you are buying each month, and this is a great way to finally see where you can cut down. Most people will tell you that it is impossible for them to save money because they never buy anything big or beyond their means. However, what they don't see are all the little items they are spending on each day that don't feel like a lot at the time but that all add up in the end. That's why keeping a tally of exactly where your money is going will make you far more aware of what you are spending money on and where you can save. It may seem like a lot of work but if you have an easy process than it really becomes nothing more than habit. And if you want to save money then you need to start becoming as aware as possible.

There are also a lot of apps for your phone or tablet that will help with tracking your expenses. They will likely also give you nice graphs for each day, week, and month that allows you to track your spending by category. If you don't have a budget app or spreadsheet to keep track of your purchases, I really recommend one! This has saved me personally a lot of money just by keeping me aware.

Tip #12: Change your phone plan

Are you on the right phone plan? You are more than likely spending far more on your phone bills each month then you need to, simply because you are on the wrong plan. Everyone is different so it's important to find one that suits you. Do you text more than you call? Do you call more than you text? Do you make your calls more at night or are you a day time caller? How much of your data plan do you really use? There are so many different ways in which you could be saving money simply by knowing the type of phone user you are and making sure your plan fits in with your lifestyle. Some people actually benefit more from prepaid phones rather than being on a contract, so it's good to check that out to in order to see what suits you best. Choose something that suits you and remember to read all the terms and conditions to make sure there are no hidden costs that you are unaware of. Never walk into a shop and take the first phone with the first plan that you see. Shop around, be inquisitive and make sure that you get all the information before purchasing. Don't be afraid to compare as many different channels as possible and to tell them that you are doing so. It's important that people see that you are someone that cannot be taken advantage of.

Tip #13: Keep your pocket change

I used to have a friend that would constantly have loose change in his pocket, on his desk, in his car and in between in couches. We used to laugh at him and tell him that if we ever needed some money all we had to do was look around his house. But this type of behaviour is actually a terrible habit to cultivate. Firstly it means that you are not respecting your money, and you're viewing loose change as something of an annoyance. You'd rather throw it away then keep it all together in one place. Secondly it means that you are sitting on a small fortune without even realizing it. You wonder why you never have enough money for anything when you're practically throwing it away. The best thing to do is to simply have a tin where you can throw your money in. At the end of the day you can rid your pockets or your wallet of all loose change and throw it into the tin. Write a date on the tin (say for 6 months to a year later) and on that day you can open it and spoil yourself with something that you've been wanting. You'll be surprised at just how much you have managed to save by doing this. I have literally been able to go on nice vacations, or had all my Christmas money sorted out at the end of the year just because I took the time to keep all my change rather than discarding it like it wasn't worth a thing. Just because it doesn't look like much at the time, doesn't mean that every day it won't add up to quite a lot!

Tip #14: Are you on the right insurance?

Insurance in your health, life and car is of course important, and if needed can save you a lot of money when you need it. However, because there is so much on offer and so many different types of insurance options available it can become quite confusing and certainly very daunting. Once again it boils down to the individual and their lifestyle. It's important to shop around and to talk to as many brokers and people as possible so that you can get all the information before making a decision. Speak to everyone and ask as many questions as possible. When it comes to your insurance you should be on a higher deductible plan in order to lower your rates. This is especially true for things like life insurance for people who are in good health and unlikely to die in the near future.

Also, be sure to look into what you can have removed from your insurance safely that will greatly reduce your rates. For example, for your car, you may be enrolled in a Collision and Comprehensive plan that covers damage to only your car in the event that you cause an accident. If your car isn't worth too much and you own it in full (you aren't paying on a loan) and you are a generally safe driver, by cancelling your Collision and Comprehensive coverage you can save yourself anywhere from $600 to $1200 a year. Even in the event of an accident that you cause, over the long term, it would likely be more cost effective to cancel this insurance type.

Along with the above, be sure to consider what each part of your insurance covers and ask questions of your agent if you do not know. Be sure, however, to do your own research into what is absolutely necessary for your lifestyle. Insurance agents want to sell you as much insurance as they can and will convince you that every type is worth having. By doing your own research, you can determine small changes you can make to your policy that can save you thousands from year to year.

Tip #15: If isn't broken, don't fix it

How often do you get a new phone or a new TV, or new clothes? I can almost bet you that most of the time you are replacing items that are in perfectly good working condition. Why are you replacing them? Because you want to have the latest gadget or a change in wardrobe, that's why. Even if you won't admit it to yourself. More than likely you'll come up with a reason for why it needs replacing. Look, we've all been there. It's hard not to get swept up in a world that is constantly telling you that what you have or how you look is not good enough. We are constantly buying things with the notion that we NEED it, when really we don't need it at all and we simply want it. Marketing companies are good at what they do, and can make you want just about anything. It always boils down to the want versus need dilemma. Unless something is broken or too outdated for the purposes that you need them for, then keep it for as long as you can. The problem with trying to keep up with all the latest gadgets is that you will literally never stop replacing and never stop spending money. That's how they make things nowadays. When you buy something there is more than likely already a better version created, just waiting to be released. Take pleasure in what you already have and keep reminding yourself as to what is important and what isn't in life. The good feelings you get from buying the latest and greatest of anything are only temporary. Is that temporary happiness worth hundreds of dollars in the long term when there is simply so much in life around you that can give you lasting happiness? Always keep in mind what it is you want versus what you need and focus on buying the things you really need.

Tip #16: If it is broken, try to fix it yourself

Of course the key word in this tip is 'try', because of course you are not going to be able to fix everything. However, there are many items in your life that you could probably fix without having to replace them completely. I mean after all, if its already broken or not working how it should, what's the worst that can happen if you tried to fix it yourself? I had a friend who would literally buy a whole new coat if her button fell off. It used to drive me insane. When I asked her why she didn't just sew a new one on she would laugh and tell me that she didn't know how to sew. If you don't know how to fix something, then see if you can learn to do it yourself. There are a huge amount of free online videos and tutorials that are there to teach you a multitude of things. This is a great opportunity to learn something new, and you might even discover something that you really enjoy or that you're really good at. Make it your goal to increase the lifespan of everything that you own, even if that means you have to fix it a few times before eventually replacing it. Don't be too quick to get rid of things simply because you want something new. Remember that at the time of buying that item it was important to you and it had value that you have perhaps forgotten about.

Tip #17: Cancel unnecessary subscriptions

How many subscriptions do you have to magazines, groups, emails and other (ahem, Netflix)? Often, at the time, we get swept up in the idea of signing up for something, especially if the cost is low. But the more we sign up for the more it adds up and most of the time we end up paying for things that we don't even use. We say yes to things because they sound good at the time but then we forget about them and we never bother to cancel. And the companies know that this happens! Do you know that most subscriptions will only stop once you cancel them, even if you only signed up for a year? Many work on a roll-over effect so that when your one year is up they will keep sending you and keep you on their database until you cancel. The best thing to do is to go through your bank statement at the end of the month and to highlight any subscriptions that you might have, and then make your way through them all and cancel them. I always tell people to instead read magazines online or only buy on the month that is has something of interest to them. Most of the time it is not necessary to buy magazines each month, especially since after a quick read you'll more than likely just throw them away. Another option for magazine is to read the article in the store without buying the copy. You get your information immediately, and you have no risk of forgetting about the magazine you just bought. You didn't have to buy anything in the first place. Not to mention most people will only read a handful of articles from any magazine they buy. Now how long would it take you to read a single page article in the store? Is that single page article worth $5+?

Tip #18: Make your own food

Don't get me wrong, I love eating out, but most of the time it's a waste of money. Also, you can often create a better (and healthier!) meal at home. Try to do the majority of cooking and meal preparation at home and you'll save so much more. Starting off with a good breakfast is not only great for your health but will also keep you full enough to stop you from rushing out to buy something from the shop. It's important to make sure that you always have snacks and meals ready so that you are not left hungry. When you're hungry you won't bother with making your own meal, especially when going to buy something that is already made is so much more convenient. Make it your priority to cook your own meals and remember that this doesn't have to be fancy or take too long. There are hundreds of online resources if you need help with how to create quick and easy meals. Keep healthy snacks such as nuts, fruit or popcorn nearby so that you have something to eat in between your meals. Then when it comes to your evening meal, try to make a few big meals in which you can either freeze or have for the next few nights. Cooking in bulk is a great way of making sure your all your ingredients get used, and you'll find that you save so much more money this way. Plus if you have a busy lifestyle, having a few freezer ready meals will save you a huge amount of time. Another great idea when it comes to making your own food is to actually plant and grow your own vegetable garden. You actually don't need a lot of space or time for this, because just a few simple pots will do. Grow some herbs to use in your meals, or plant some tomato seeds and watch them grow.

You'll be able to keep growing and using these which will save you huge amounts on your weekly shopping.

Packing your own food for lunches or other meals is not just good for your daily lifestyle but also something to consider when going on a trip. Road trip food can often end up being unhealthy and expensive, so instead pack your own and save yourself a lot of money this way. Sure beats having McDonalds kill you and your wallet slowly but surely!

Tip #19: There's nothing wrong with second-hand stores

Have you heard the saying, 'Once person's rubbish is another person's treasure'? There is absolutely nothing wrong with shopping at a second-hand store and you might be surprised at what you find! This is a great way of saving money and you can often find items almost as good as new. Trust me; nobody will know where you bought it from so it really doesn't matter at all. I have actually found that some of my best purchases have been from second-hand stores, especially furniture which can often be a lot more unique than ones you'd find new in a shop. It is also a great place to look for old books and games for the home, because these are items that don't have to be new for you to enjoy them.

Tip #20: Be careful of stress or emotional spending

A lot of people buy whenever they feel stressed or emotional as a way to pick themselves up again. This is one of the worst times to buy because you are not thinking clearly and you will more than likely buy things that you don't really need at all. Once again they will make you happy for just that short time, but anything that adds to your debt will simply get you feeling stressed and emotional again. Don't try to justify your stress spending just because of a bad day or a bad experience. There are other ways of feeling better that will last a lot longer than a poor purchase choice. It's good to be aware of times like this and to take a step back from the situation when it happens. Knowing that you are something that tends to buy when stressed or unhappy is the first step in making sure you don't fall into the trap again. When you find yourself feeling this way then make sure you have a fall back action. Go for a walk or a run – getting some exercise will clear your head and help you to think more clearly. Plus the endorphins released will get rid of the stress and get you feeling happy again. Phone a friend or a loved one – tell them beforehand that you might be calling them when the urge to spend comes along and ask them to please help you when you do. Sometimes simply talking to someone helps you to see things differently. Do something you enjoy such as reading, watching a movie or doing a hobby – it's good to take your mind off your problems sometimes by doing something that you enjoy. Whatever you do just don't buy when you are stressed or emotional. You'll only be adding to your debt and creating more problems for yourself down the line.

Tip #21: Buy in bulk

Buying in bulk is generally a lot cheaper than single items and a great way of saving money in the long run. Make a list of all your items that you use on a more regular basis and then price these at the shop as single items and as bulk items. If the bulk items work out cheaper than this is the route to go. Of course always make sure that you do not buy any food items that may spoil, so check the expiry dates before doing so. Otherwise the whole object of buying in bulk will be defeated. When it comes to bulk it is also great to cook in bulk. On a Sunday I like to create two big meals and then freeze them. Ingredients will go a lot further in one big meal then in a few separate ones so it's a great way to save money and time during the week. Also having some meals all ready for you in the freezer means that you won't be tempted to rush out to buy a take-out on the nights that you are too busy to cook. The more food that you can prepare for the week in one go, the better. It might mean a few hours are taken up of your day but you'll actually save time throughout the week because of it. Either way it's a win-win situation, both time and money saved in this process.

Tip #22: Quit smoking

I say this for both the health of your body, your mind and your pocket. When I quit smoking I finally realized just what damage it was doing to me. With the health issues aside I was astonished as to how much money was going towards a rather destroying habit. Do yourself a favour and take some time to calculate roughly how much you would save a year if you had to quit. Be honest with how much you have a day and then calculate a rough figure for the year. It might not seem like a lot each day but when you see how much you'd save over a full year you might reconsider. When you quit put that money aside and watch it grow. Not only will it make the process of quitting a lot easier but you'll also be able to put that money to a much better use at the end of the year. There are many online resources to help you through the quitting process as well as many support groups you can attend. It's not an easy road to be on, but at the end you'll know it was worth doing.

Tip #23: Choose your bank wisely

Is your bank account the best for you? Most of us don't think much about the pros and cons of which banks to use when opening up an account. Often, our parents open it up for us and we then never bother to change. Or else, we go on a recommendation by someone else and never really look into it ourselves. Do you use your card a lot? Or do you tend to draw out money more than using a card? There are different charges for all different types of transactions so be sure to find out what you use the most and then to find out which bank can offer you the lowest transaction rate. Additionally, your bank may charge you monthly or yearly fees for not maintaining a certain balance or for not having a certain number of transactions.

These banks are terrible and they eat away at your money slowly but surely. There are more than enough banks out there that offer free checking and savings with no strings attached or any hidden fees. Seek those out to save yourself a little money each year. Once again, it's a case of a small figure that you tend to ignore but that over time builds up to quite a large amount.

Tip #24: Use the library

When's the last time you used the library? More and more people have stopped going to the library and choose instead to buy new books at the shops. The thing with books is this – you are more than likely only going to read that book once. After that the book will sit on a shelf, unused, for years to come. Now don't get me wrong, I'm a massive book lover myself and an avid reader, but I've had to stop myself from spending too much at shops for something I'm really not going to use all that much. Because, let's face it, books are not cheap. Instead, I visit the library or read books on Kindle. This is a great way to find a wide variety of books that you might never have picked up before. Plus it's free or a fraction of the cost. I generally get myself a few books each month, and if I find one that I absolutely love and want to own then I either buy it or I put it on my Christmas wish list. I know so few people that visit the library and instead spend so much money on books, magazines, movies, etc. The library is a beautiful place to spend some time with books and surround yourself with stories and ideas. There is also something incredibly special about a book that has passed through many hands, and I think it's something that we need to revive again. Don't waste your money on things you are not going to use more than once. And if you're looking for a place to simply get away and find some peace and quiet, then the library is the place to be.

Tip #25: Check your tires

The more un-inflated your tires on your car are, the more gas mileage you will lose. Such a simple little trick that can go a very long way when it comes to money saving. Every time you go to fill up on gas just make sure that your tires are pumped to the recommended tire pressure. Most people don't pump their tires until the very last minute which means they are constantly using more gas than they need to. Check your manual to find out exactly what your tires should be pumped to and then just make a habit to check as often as you can. Don't waste money on something as simple as a deflated tire.

Also, be sure that your car's tires are aligned properly. If they aren't aligned, over time you will see uneven wear in the tread which leads to them needing to be replaced more frequently. And if you have ever needed tires replaced, you know it's not a cheap investment. If you have your tires aligned properly, you also save on gas because your car is fighting less friction as you drive.

Tip #26: Turn off and unplug

If you're not using an appliance, then switch it off and unplug. It's these little things that all add and could be saving you a fortune. Most of the time half the things you are paying for in your electricity bill could be avoided, and all it takes is a quick moment to unplug. It's a great habit to get into so if you do it often enough it won't even seem like an issue anymore. It will just become part of your daily routine. I know people who leave their television sets on all day simply because they like noise around, even though most of the time they are not even watching it. Switching off the TV will not only save your electricity bill but also give you some much needed time for self-reflection and the opportunity to spend your time on other more uplifting activities. Another very good reason to unplug is to avoid any damage that could be caused by a power surge. This can happen for many different reasons including bad weather conditions or a simple and unavoidable electrical fault. If this happens you could end up paying far more in repairs or replacements.

Tip #27: Invest your money

Investing your money is one of the best ways to see the biggest growth in your money, and if you do it wisely you can save far more than you are right now. Investing is a clever way to make sure you are making the most of your savings each month. The trick, of course, is where to invest, how much to invest, and how to go about it. Speak to your broker, or financial advisor to find out what will work best for you. Also speak to people around you such as friends, family and work colleagues to find out what they are doing and what advice they can offer you. A few things to keep in mind:

- Invest a minimum of 10% of your income by creating an automated system which will deduct that money off each month. If you have to put the money in yourself each month you will more than likely either forget about it or you'll find other ways to spend that money. If you have it automatically set up you will completely forget about it and your savings will start to add up nicely. Most banks will help with this. As will most employers. Set up direct deposit where you can.
- If you're going to invest in stocks, then make sure you research it thoroughly before doing so. While you can make a lot of money this way, you can also lose a lot of money. So it's very important to know what you doing. Also be careful of just investing on one individual stock because if you lose out then you lose out completely.
- Don't invest in anything if you don't understand it. Ask as many questions as you want and research as much as you can. But definitely be willing to take time to check out all your options and see what works with your risk tolerance.

- Be patient. Investing (correctly) doesn't mean you'll be rich overnight, however it is a nice steady way of getting more from your money over time.
- Look into mutual funds such as Vanguard. There are thousands of others out there with varying risk levels and pay-out levels. Some will even pay dividends every so many months. Since these are managed by professionals who often invest themselves in their own mutual fund, they want to make sure the fund succeeds. They lose business if it doesn't. Mutual funds allow you to put your money away into something that grows steadily over time more often than not, and the best part is you don't even have to manage it! So research mutual funds and see if this is something you'd be interested in trying out!
- IRA's are a fantastic way to save for retirement. They are like a savings account and a mutual fund combined. You put money in on a regular basis and watch it grow over months to years without you having to lift a finger. Your employer may also have a program where they contribute to your IRA as well, which often amounts to matching what you contribute every pay check. It is very much like a savings account because in many IRA programs you can withdrawal the money you invested at any time (but not the capital gains from your investment) in case you need it. Even if you put your latte money into your IRA every single day, and if you start early enough, you can retire a

millionaire (I'm not lying or exaggerating at all!). Check into the retirement plans that your employer offers and see what they contribute. Also, determine what you can contribute to it as well.

- If you commit to not letting your money sit in a checking account, but instead letting it work for you, in the long run, you will have more than you know what to do with. Consider all investment options and see what works for you. Do not be intimidated by the lingo and the jargon of the financial world. It is complicated at first, but well worth the time looking into (considering it can leave you retiring with millions if you do it right).

Tip #28: Find free events

You don't have to spend a lot of money to have fun. There are plenty of things you can do that don't cost anything. It's also a great excuse to get outdoors as much as possible and to enjoy nature the way it was intended. Go hiking, go for a run, go for a picnic, play a sport etc. The whole world is waiting for you to enjoy it. Have friends over for a bring and share dinner, and enjoy an evening of food and games together. Some of my most memorable moments are simply the times spent with friends, and not the money spent on things. Use your online resources to scout for free events happening in your city. It's a great way to get more involved in the community and to enjoy the free resources that are available to you. You'll discover a whole new world of people who are doing exactly the same as you!

During seasons such as winter or summer, it can be a good idea to set your in-home thermostat to something closer to the temperature outside. This way, your air conditioner or heater isn't working as hard (i.e. using less electricity or fuel) to keep your house at a constant temperature. By no means am I recommending *matching* the outside temperature or making it ridiculously cold or hot depending on the season. Just simply turning down the heat a few degrees during the winter or turning down the AC during the summer can shave a lot off your electric bill each month.

Tip #29: Ask for help

Are you ashamed of your debt or money management habits? Because debt is something that happens slowly it can often be a hard thing to admit even to yourself. I remember meeting a guy once who refused to let anyone pay for anything. No matter where we went or what we did he would be adamant that he was the one to pay. It was obvious that he was showing off but we all naturally assumed that he at least had the money to do so. Only months down the line we discovered that he was completely in debt and had absolutely no real money to his name. He just didn't want anyone to know. This is the case with a lot of people who want to appear in a certain way rather than admit to others that they are having a problem with money. Most people find it embarrassing and they would rather pretend to those around them than admit defeat. This can cause a huge amount of stress on a person and it is incredibly damaging to their well-being. It's important to be honest with people and to find the courage to ask for help. You'll be surprised at how many people are either going through the same thing as you or at how many people have been there before. It turns out very few people are good at managing their money! Having a support group can be hugely beneficial when you are trying to become debt-free. Be honest and open with those around you and ask them for their suggestions and their support. If you don't have anyone to talk to you or you simply don't want to speak to those around you then turn to online resources for help. There are plenty online places where you can seek advice and many success stories from people who have been through exactly the same thing as you.

Tip #30: Make your own gifts

Make your own gifts as often as you can. Not only will this save you a lot of money but it can often be a much more thoughtful and appreciative gift. It also gives you a great opportunity to have fun and be creative which most people do not make enough time for these days. If you don't want to create your own gift or if you simply do not have the time or energy to do so then try to be resourceful when it comes to the wrapping or cards. Reuse paper, keep gift bags, and use things like newspaper to wrap your gifts. You can still make the gift look beautiful without spending too much on the gift wrapping. Also remember that it's what's inside that counts, because even if the person loves the wrapping paper that is still the part that is going to be thrown away. The same goes for cards, a simple note to say who the gift is from will suffice. Keep it simple, and remember what's important. I can assure you that some of my greatest gifts are those made from the heart and not those that cost the most. Society has taught us that we have to show off with big and expensive presents, when this is really not the case. Go back to basics and go back to the heart.

Tip #31: Be thankful for what you have

The last tip is one of great simplicity and yet holds the biggest importance of all. One of the top reasons that people are in debt is simply because they are always looking for more without looking at what they already have. They constantly want bigger and better things and forget how to appreciate the life that they have. They look for joy in material goods rather than in themselves, in the people around them and in experiences. They have forgotten what true happiness is all about, and because of this they believe that they can buy it. One of the best money saving tips I can give you today is to be thankful for what you already have. Every day, make a list of what you are grateful for, no matter how clichéd this may sound. By acknowledging this on a daily basis you'll be more inclined to take note of what is around you. Be thankful for all that you have and enjoy your life. I promise you this; there are more important things in life than material goods. Life is there to be explored and enjoyed, and once you rid yourself of your debt you'll find freedom that you never knew before.

Conclusion

Money doesn't have to ruin your life. You don't have to live your entire life in debt, stressed and unhappy with how things have spiralled. Instead, you can take back the control and live a life of financial freedom. The biggest problem that people have when finding themselves in debt is that they feel overwhelmed by the problem and unsure of how to solve it. Instead of looking at the bigger picture, you need to break down your debt into smaller and more manageable solutions. You can therefore start to slowly chip away at your debt bit by bit until suddenly it's not a problem anymore. By looking at the 30 tips and tricks you'll see that each tip is something that you can do TODAY. While each of these consists of small habits to incorporate into your life, the repercussions of them will be huge later down the line, and soon you'll be out of your debt. Once you're out of debt you can start concentrating on managing this type of lifestyle and you'll finally find that you are able to save. Having savings will quite literally change your life forever. You'll be able to do the things that you want to do and go to the places you want to go, and you'll have a fall back plan in case anything goes wrong. All of this IS achievable. I know it's achievable because it's something that I have personally gone through myself, and I know countless people that will tell you the same. It's nothing to be ashamed about, and there are far more people going through the same problem than you think. So decide right now that you're going to make it happen and you WILL. Financial freedom is waiting for you.

Thank you for taking the time to read through this book. By simply reading these tips you have already taken the first step towards a debt free life. So right now, take a deep breath and close your eyes. Envision the life that you have always wanted, without debt and without stress. Open your eyes. You can make this come true, starting today!

Remember:

Tip #1: Credit Card – You only need the one
Tip #2: Be shop smart
Tip #3: Know the sales
Tip #4: Don't shop on an empty stomach
Tip #5: Your home doesn't have to be big
Tip #6: Before buying, ask yourself 'do I really need this?'
Tip #7: Name brands are NOT important
Tip #8: Drink coffee at home
Tip #9: Cash is king
Tip #10: Have a monthly budget
Tip #11: Know where your money is going
Tip #12: Change your phone plan
Tip #13: Keep your pocket change
Tip #14: Are you on the right insurance?
Tip #15: If isn't broken, don't fix it
Tip #16: If it is broken, try to fix it yourself
Tip #17: Cancel unnecessary subscriptions
Tip #18: Make your own food
Tip #19: There's nothing wrong with second-hand stores
Tip #20: Be careful of stress or emotional spending

Tip #21: Buy in bulk
Tip #22: Quit smoking
Tip #23: Choose your bank wisely
Tip #24: Use the library
Tip #25: Check your tires
Tip #26: Turn off and unplug
Tip #27: Invest your money
Tip #28: Find free events
Tip #29: Ask for help
Tip #30: Make your own gifts
Tip #31: Be thankful for what you have

I wish you all the best of luck with your new journey.

Become the master of your own fate, and take back your money control!

If you found this book valuable or helpful, be sure to leave a review on Amazon. I thank you so much in advance for all your support of "The Productive Minimalist" E-book series.

 If you are interested in other Minimalist Lifestyle Strategies, be sure to check out the first book in this series:

"Simply Clutter Free Living: 25 Simple Tips to Organize Your Life and Enhance Productivity"

Which can be found at the following link via Amazon:
http://amzn.to/1IvfWNr